MAKE LOVE NOT DINNER

By Shay Delady

‘One million people commit suicide every year’
The World Health Organization

Published by
Chipmunkapublishing
PO Box 6872
Brentwood
Essex CM13 1ZT
United Kingdom

http://www.chipmunkapublishing.com

Introduction

Shay is one of the top escorts in London. Born in a well to do family, Shay went to private school and then obtained her higher studies in the USA. She has a Masters degree in Management and worked in an Investment Bank for few years. Tired of long hours and number crunching Shay decided to change her lifestyle and obtained diploma in beauty and massage with a vision to involve more artistic elements in her life. At the same time she came out of a sour relationship giving her the opportunity to completely alter her life around.
Shay decided to work for herself on her terms, as she embarked on a solo journey that led her to the unknown and often feared path of high class escorting. The new path, new place and new lifestyle had given her the daily hands-on enlightenment on complicated human psychology and varied physical desires. This was a line of living that could be quite glamorous yet dark and lonely at times but experiences can be used to learn the lesson on life through trial, strength of mind, laughter, and tears.

In Shay's Book 'Make Love Not Dinner' we get the first hand sexual knowledge and life advice from an escort who made herself successful in the competitive London scene and been featured in TV documentaries. She has written the book based on her vast intimate experiences with men from around the world to realistically enhance people's sexuality as well as lifestyle in our modern busy world. The book also features top sexual fantasies that clients shared with Shay, with a touch of humour. It discusses her experiences to offer guidance and sex techniques to people to overcome low self esteem, ensuring dating success, reigniting long term relationships etc through self development and improved sexual performance. Whether you are a beginner or a veteran, 'Make Love Not Dinner' will give you new ideas to play with.

James

There is a knock on the door, my heart pounds a little. A man I have never met is standing on the other side. I check myself for the final time and open the door smilingly wearing perfume, black jewelled stilettos, low cut black lace lingerie with a red bow tie in the back and a lace thong. I have soft makeup on with smoky eyes and glossy lips. My hair is loose, falling down to my bare mid back. A handsome man around 45 years in a smart business suit walks in. I greet him with a kiss on his lips. He introduces himself as 'James'. His eyes lit up as he looks up and down my body and I can sense how much he wants me. He has discreetly come to spend intimate time with me on his lunch hour. He has seen my photos on the internet, but the fact that he has no idea what I will wear or smell like makes it all the more seductive. I sit him down and offer him a drink. He slips me the envelope with my fee in it. We kiss passionately on the sofa with our hands running all over each other's body and hair. I take his coat and tie off and lead him to my bedroom.

The bedside lamps are dimmed, curtains closed, sensual oil burners give the room a sexy feeling. I slowly unbutton James' shirt, kissing him on his neck, chest, running my tongue slowly. He moans with pleasure. He kisses my nipples through the lacy lingerie and gently touches me inside my thongs to feel my wetness. I take his trousers off and ask him on get in the bed. Then I touch his back and sides very softly just with the tips of my fingers almost like touching with a feather. Then I focus on the sensual points of his body. I go behind him pressing my soft breasts against his back. I firmly kiss from the nape of his neck straight down his spine all the way to the bum and touch them with my fingertips in circular motion. I flick my tongue between his bum and just under them. I continue to run my fingertips on back of his thighs down to his ankles circling around the ankles and between the toes. I lick firmly on back of his knees and around his ankle. James has his back towards me so he has no idea where I will touch him next. This adds an element of surprise for him turning him on even more. I move on to his balls barely touching them from behind. I put my fingers in my mouth to get them wet. Then I run my wet fingers around his balls. Sides of balls are extremely sensual. James moans loudly as I continue to torture him in the most excruciating sensuous way.

Slowly I turn James over to reveal how much he has wanted me! He takes my clothes off. I kiss his ears, brush my cheeks on his and kiss him on his lips. I then kiss him on the front of his neck right below the Adam's apple. I flick my tongue on his nipples down his belly button. I kiss the inside of his elbow using pressure with my tongue then move down to softly lick between the knuckles. By now James is craving to make love to me but I make him wait. The best is yet to come! I move my fingers slowly upwards James' legs to sensually touch his inner thighs.

Then I finally take him in my mouth. James cries in pleasure. I gently tap the tip of his penis with my tongue. Then I swirl my tongue around the tip. I move downwards flicking my tongue down his shaft. I take my out and flick and roll his balls with my tongue. I take him in my mouth again. This time I swirl my tongue all the way down his penis clock wise and come up till the tip anti clockwise. The sensations created by the transition between clockwise and anti clockwise motions drive him mad. After few minutes of sucking, who is by now more than ready to be inside me! I put my finger in my vagina and make James taste my sweetness. He gets greedy and puts his tongue in me to taste me amorously.

Finally I get on top of James and slide him inside my wet pussy. I lean forward so my breasts reach his mouth. I sit up straight to give him the full view. I touch my neck and breasts, run my hand through my hair, put my finger in my mouth. These visual effects are extremely effective with men. We change positions. James gets on top, deep inside me and we make love till he reaches climax. James is a regular client now and says that it was the most sensuous and amazing sex he has ever had!

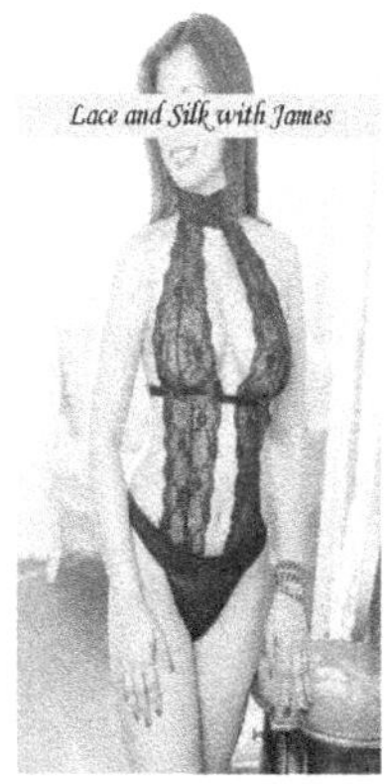

GUIDE FOR WOMEN:

Every woman desires to know the secrets of good lovemaking to amaze her man. Women crave to hear their men say that she is the best sexual partner he has ever had. Escorting has given me the opportunity to make love with many men. My vast intimate experience with men from various age, ethnic group, religion and professional background has given me the insight of male psychology on sexual encounters. The secret behind knowing a man's body is, knowing his mind. If you know how to turn his mind on, his body will follow. I am sharing my experience and expertise here, not only to arm women with techniques to know men but to make you feel sexy as a woman and become the object of desire.

Secret 1: Knight in Shining Armour

Treat a man in bed as if he is the God's gift to the world, wrapped in blue ribbon. Every man's deepest desire is to be the knight in shining armour in the eyes of his woman. When a gentleman walks in through the door of an escort, he gets treated as if he is THE god-send work of art, the ultimate fantasy of the woman.

Sex is not only for a man to enjoy and woman to go along. The more a woman enjoys the sex the more her man will enjoy too. Keep in mind that a man is making love with you, not to you. If you make a man feel worthy, he would be eager to please you more. Look at him up and down with lust and admire him as you get close to him. Focus on the positive aspects of his body and skill. Whisper how nice he smells or how much you love to run your hands through his hair. Later on when your time comes, he will return you the compliment. He might even agree to change his style for you which you have nagging him to do for the past ten years, unsuccessfully!! Besides, follow the golden rule, as you would like to be treated as a goddess by him later. Contrary to popular belief, men are actually far more nervous about sex and performance than women.

One day I asked 'James' how felt when he knocked on my door for the first time. He said that he was standing outside the door for what seemed like an hour, in reality it was the longest ten seconds of his life, his heart was pounding. Until that moment everything had been so easy, I guess the beauty of the internet was finished, this was real life. He stared at the door, knew exactly where the bell was, it was parallel to where his heart should have been, beating normally, instead it was beating so loudly he imagined the street was listening. He moved forward and knocked so lightly that nobody could have heard and the door swung open to reveal a beautiful woman in an outfit that took his breath away. The sensuous negligee accentuated every curve in a body which was both perfect yet somehow reassuring. As he was led to my sofa and kissed in a gentle but sexual way, the wetness of my tongue gave an invitation to an afternoon of passion and ultimately the most fulfilling sex of his life.

He is an experienced man with plenty of conquests to his credit but this was unlike anything that had happened before, as he was swept along on a swell of passion into an uncontrollable state of mind prepared to commit to anything to satisfy my urges and respond to the gentle but demanding probing of my fingers, my tongue and the firm and erect nipples which were demanding to be sucked.

As I took him to the bed removing my clothes and roughly unbuttoning his shirt as if I could not wait to touch his body, my desires were evident. He tasted the wetness of my womanhood as I asked him to enter me. It was the most passionate moment of his life as I was totally in control. I whispered in his ear and told him to make love to me hard and gave out little cries of ecstasy which drove him crazy. He was being swept into a world he did not know existed and could not get enough. It was a drug, the most powerful aphrodisiac and made him feel like a giant.

When I took him in my mouth he thought he was about to burst, it was the most expert blow job he had ever received and soon gave up the unequal struggle. We made love in every conceivable position and he exploded inside me and screamed as every fibre in his body was stretched to breaking point. He was exhausted and sunk into my arms seeking reassurance and wanting to feel safe and comforted. It was a feeling so incredible, he knew he would want more from this "mysterious lady who knew so much about life".

Secret 2: Element of Surprise

Men love to be surprised. It triggers their need for variety in sex life. Most men go to escorts not because they have stopped loving their wives or girlfriends. In fact men love them enough to remain committed to them and not have an affair. Men can separate love and sex. Going to escort is an emotionally detached way of fulfilling sexual desires. Most of this desire is generated by the need for variety. Being with the same woman year after year can be boring for a man. This is the main reason behind men in their forties onwards visiting escorts more often than their younger counterparts. Try to provide your life with variety. Do not just limit sex in bed every Saturday night for fifteen minutes in the same position. Dare to be unpredictable. One day, get dressed in super sexy lingerie/ costume, high heels, perfume and open the door when your man arrives at home and watch his jaw drop. He will never mistake you as his predictable, boring wife. In fact he would be a little scared thinking that you might have your own agenda! Men are visual creatures, so, white tunic and khaki trousers day after day will not do it for them! One of the main reasons of male excitement when they knock on an escort's door is the anticipation of the unknown. When a man is on the way to meet an escort, half the excitement is the guessing how the lady will prepare herself like for him.

The next day when he is at his work, sitting amongst his colleagues, send him a very illicit text message explaining in detail how much you enjoyed the sex with him the night before or mail him some very sexy photos of yourself, like I do with my very special clients. He will be very horny but would not be able act on it. So he will be thinking about you all afternoon. One day call him and tell him how much you want him right at that moment. Remember how you always want him to come home to you? Well, that day, he will ignore his friends at pub or even the Chelsea – Manchester United match because he cannot wait to come home to YOU!

Secret 3: Have Sex Then Dinner

Do not worry about the household chores the minute you come home from work. Once in a while, try to take a break and focus on yourself and your partner rather than on your laundry. Work is stressful enough. If you further stress yourselves out by talking about bills, problems of commuting etc then it creates an environment of tension and subsequently kills the mood. Eventually the feelings of negativity and problems consume the intimate life. Arguments tend to have a snowballing effect, at the end neither recalling what the initial argument was about, but the bitter words exchanged linger for a long time to come. When relationships reach the end, people look back and wish a thousand things they had done differently. So relax, make love, and then worry about the cooking and dishwashing. Nobody will complain!

Escorts offer a domesticity free environment where men see us as goddesses by the bed with no ironing boards, nappies or rubber gloves in sight. However make believe it is, it does give a refreshing time out for both partners. Do not ruin your present worrying about the future.

Secret 4: Create a Sexy Ambience

Buy some sensuous aromatic jasmine or lavender candles and burners to decorate your place. It is both relaxing and seductive. Besides, everyone looks better in candle light! Fluff up your bed with exotic pillow cases. Then slip into something sexy, turn on lounge style music and open a bottle of wine. Allow yourself to feel like Venus herself!

I understand that it is difficult to switch off from kids, diapers, cooking and think of 'home' as sex heaven. Escorts also deal with everyday household chores and sometimes even children. It is not realistic that you can only be sexy when you are whisked away for luxury holiday. So try to make good use of your lovely bedroom right at home. In fact keep the bedroom out of domestic arena and create it into your sanctuary for relaxation and lovemaking so when you walk into it, you would immediately feel free of daily chaos as you do when you enter your favourite spa. Try to look decent when you are at home with your partner, your hot everyday date.

Secret 5: Train Your Voice

Sometimes unknowingly we women speak at a high pitched voice in person or over the phone. Remember, deep husky voice is considered sexy by the opposite sex. There is no need to copy the sex chat line operators! Speak naturally, just a little softer. It will add mystery to your presence. Sexy voice can be just as much a turn on as a sexy body. Imagine the power to make a man you have not or will not ever meet fantasize about you just after talking to you over the phone! When a gentleman calls an escort, he makes his decision within first few seconds of talking to the lady. Invitation blended with mystery sprinkled with cheerfulness, is the recipe to unleash the male mental passion. After a few days of practice, the new voice will become the real voice!

Secret 6: Feel Sexy

You can only be sexy in somebody else's eyes if you are confident about your own sexuality first. Do not be shy to put on a classy dress just hinting your cleavage, sophisticated high heels and sip champagne at a bar by yourself. Keep it all elegant, (no mini dress with stocking suspender showing)… men do not find desperate women interesting. Before you notice, you would have a long queue of admirers. Sure there will always be people to snare at you, but remember, the sheer fact that they are giving energy to you means you are igniting their jealousy. It only proves they wish they were like you! Besides do not be trapped by dogma and fear of others' opinions. Doing so will only make you end up living others' life. In the process you would forget your own dreams and plans for life. So make your own plan and have the courage to be a leader.

Know that the key to your sexual ignition is not between your legs, it is inside your head. The brain is person's biggest sex organ, sending nerve impulses running down the spinal cord to trigger an arousal. Once I saw a man I fancied at a bar, I got a sit where I was highly visible, and then I played a fantasy in my mind about him. It did not take him long to sense and come up to me... but in case he did not have the courage, I would have gone up and said hello.

So next time you go out, dress to impress and when you see a man you fancy, just walk up and introduce yourself. Stand next to him and start by a smile, a nice smile is always an ice-melter. Being shy is no longer a virtue. You have nothing to loose. In case you do not like him after two minutes, you can always walk away gracefully. If ever a man asks for my number which I did not wish to provide him with, I politely decline in return asking him to give me his number instead.

Secret 7: Think of Yourself as Sexy

We women tend to find faults with ourselves every time we put on a sexy outfit or see ourselves naked in the mirror. I can vouch from my experience that men are not at all concerned about one stray hair your beautician missed on your eyebrow. Men are more into women who enjoy uninhibited sex.

You do not have to be 34D-24-34 with mile-long legs to be sexy. Sexiness is all in your mind. Try to emphasise on more attractive parts of your body and downplay the least attractive. Such as if you are busty but your bum is a little too big, then wear a dress that is low cut to enhance your cleavage yet loose waist down to conceal your lower body. On the other hand put on a close neck mini dress if your breasts are small but legs are slim.

Lots of women often do not feel confident about their body after childbirth. But with a little bit of effort pre-pregnancy body can be regained. Meanwhile if you are suffering from low self esteem, choose outfits and positions that make your body look flattering. Missionary, doggy style positions will make your tummy look flatter. On the other hand if you are worried about your bum, then sitting on top of him will make your bum invisible to your man.

It is common misperception that men like super skinny women who look like boys. In fact the most successful courtesans are curvy and men cannot have enough of their bodies!

Secret 8: Self Development

Taking care of yourself, inside and out, body and mind, is the secret of being attractive in your own mind and others. It takes just as long to put on something unattractive as it does to wear something nice and coordinated. In fact your mind is able to pick things up faster if they are coordinated. When you are wearing something simple black, just accessorize it with a nice belt, scarf or a single elegant pearl strand. Spend ten minutes in the morning putting on a soft makeup and doing your hair, it will make your day noticeably different, a coat of mascara certainly would not hurt. Always wear matching, flattering bra and knickers set, as you never know how your day might turn in the evening. Make sure your shoes match your bags. Do not keep items in the closet with tags on for months. Fashion changes very fast and you do not want to be the last one wearing or worse wearing so late that it is in last years magazine, when you paid just as much as everybody else for it. Even if you are not exactly into trends, and prefer classic clothes that never go out of fashion, wear them when you buy them. When are you saving it for? 'Now' is the most special time. A simple looking woman can be strikingly attractive in ten minutes with the right clothes, makeup and accessories. Coordinated appearance reflects a coordinated mind.

Make a routine, (maybe the first day of every month or week), to get your manicure, pedicure, eyebrows, facial etc done so you are always ready to step out in style in short notice. Make sure to cleanse and moisturize your face every morning and night, no matter how rushed or tired you are, it only takes one minute. Put your clothes on so that you shine through in the true sense, do not let an expensive dress hang over you like a misplaced item. Besides, when you look coordinated and well maintained, a simple black dress goes a long way, whatever its price might be. As grooming increasingly become a part of daily plan, getting ready turns easier and less time consuming.

Do not limit your reading within ladies fashion magazine. Try to read about news around the world everyday. Keep up with the business, environment and sports news. Spend time experiencing different culture and heritage through books or travel. Do not sit around counting hours, make your hours count.

Secret 9: Hygiene & Cleanliness

Personal and feminine hygiene is one of the important aspects in male mind. Although many people often think men do not care about a woman's hygiene standard, they do… a lot. Even the most gorgeous woman would loose all appeal in an instant, if a man is put off by her greasy hair, body odour, bad breath or undesired smell in intimate part. Regardless of how long you have been with your partner, always make sure to cleanse your intimate part after sex. Immediate cleansing keeps unwanted odour at bay.

Do not assume that if you are sexy enough, men will not care about the mess in your apartment. Imagine bringing a man to your place for the first time and your worn out bra is hanging over to be the first item in sight or forcing to make love on a bed with pile of clothes. Yikes….a preview of life with you will flash through your prince's mind, severely clouding any potential for future. Messy home gives out a sign of messy life. Only men who would not mind a messy home are men with similarly messy home and lifestyle.

Make a routine of cleaning your place once a week. The easiest way to keep a home tidy is not to make a big mess in the first place. Make a habit of putting clothes back in the closet or laundry bag straight away instead of spreading them all around only to be collected later. Moreover a neat place seems more spacious. Have some fresh flowers in the living room, it will boost your mood and uplift the setting. Tidy environment generates tidy mindset.

A man does not need or want to see feminine intimate toiletries scattered around the bathroom, neither does he want to see you going through the rituals of putting on clay face mask and shaving your legs etc. So do these in your intimate privacy away from any male audience.

Secret 10: First Date

First date is all about total impression, preview of everything you are and not. This is the opportunity to establish that you offer the total package. You are a beautiful, charming, intelligent, well-conversant woman with excellent sense of style and immaculate manners (including punctuality). A combination dreamt of and treasured by the successful men with honest intention.

Dress in a classy manner, a black dress is always a safe bet if you are unsure. Ask your date ahead of time where you would be going. This will not only give you the idea on what to wear but also give him chance to prepare and know your thoughts on the venue.

Do not shy away from giving a man his due compliment. Like women, men also look for approval and commendation in the eyes of their partner on the first day and every day. If a man has made an effort for you, please let him know that you appreciate that. It will only want him to please you even more. If you have decided to go out with this man, you surely would be able to find something nice to say to him.

Table mannerism is one of the most telling signs of your level of sophistication. However accidents do happen, hence, do not let a spill hinder your ability to enjoy the experience. Just smile and get over it. The faster you move on to cheerful pasture, the faster people around you will forget about the incident.

Under no circumstance, consume more alcohol than you can handle. Getting drunk will make you loose control and do things you will feel embarrassed about later. Men like fun women, but chasing a date bouncing around the bar like a loose helium balloon is never on their wish list.

Have a 'ready-to-wear' genuine smile on your face, it is the biggest ice-breaker and the most disarming technique ever. Laugh at jokes, even if they are not very funny. Be positive in your conversations with other people and above all yourself. Negative attitude would only attract negative companions. Successful, happy people do not like negative conversations socially. Do not fear to be unique, it is the only way people will remember you. What is the fun in blending in to the extent where people cannot remember your name the next week?

Men find knowledgeable women with business acumen tremendously sexy. Do not allow your date turn into a one sided conversation, be prepared to show off your knowledge. Let your man will know that he has got one precious woman in his arms who can turn from a seductress in private to a lady in public to a sharp businesswoman in a blink of an eye. So, relax, enjoy yourself and let men want you.

Secret 11: Play Games

Make your fantasies reality. Most people are embarrassed to share their fantasies with their partners fearing rejection or laughter. Men however feel free to share their darkest fantasies with their escorts because primarily they care less about what the escort might think of them and secondarily they know that the escort most probably would agree to play out the fantasy. So, do not loose out on you man's fantasies. If he is reluctant to share with you, then you share yours first. He will follow you faster than your trained Labrador retriever ever responded to your whistle. Have a game planned in your mind. Cuff him to your bed, put a blindfold on his eyes and then tickle him with a feather any way you like. He is yours to enjoy and best of all he cannot see what treat is coming next! If you feel shy telling him your fantasies face to face, then send him an e-mail detailing what you want him to do to you. No man will turn down that invitation.

With the right plan, the unavailable and the unreachable can become very much attainable.

Secret 12: Make Use of Weekends/ Holidays

Do not spend the whole weekend cleaning your backyard wearing rubber gloves or stressing over kids. Find quality time to spend with your partner, no matter what you do. It is great if you enjoy doing household things together, but do not let minor chores take over your life and drift you two apart. Remember it is both of your weekend to enjoy. So if you in burden each other with all the stress and household chores, then you would not look forward to spend the weekend with each other. Consequently you and your partner would start to spend more time away from each other and home to be with friends outside separately. Try to get away on long weekends or holidays to somewhere new to relax and explore each other.

Make your time together count. As years pass by, you can only look back at time and think how you have used or wasted this amazing gift.

Dressing style on weekends is another important aspect. Most people tend to dress rather casually on weekends, which is absolutely fine. However remember to make an effort to look smart and sexy while you are putting on your casual outfits. You do not want to keep your worst rags for weekends as this is the time your best audience, your partner, gets to see you. We dress to impress our clients, colleagues all week long so let us make the slightest effort to impress the most important spectator.

Secret 13: Mind-blowing Blowjob Techniques

When it comes to blowjobs, do not rush in. Imagine how much time we take to make a cake to impress our mothers- in- law! So why would you treat your man's intimate part in a rush? The most important ingredient to giving an amazing blowjob is the ATTITUDE. If you consider blowjob as 'work' with no enthusiasm, then do not bother performing the act. If you put him in your mouth up and down with no vibration, variation, passion and cannot wait it to be over, then the man will sense that you are doing it out of duty, thus he will not enjoy either. Remember that positive attitude will make up for any lack of technique. Keep in mind that arousal is an electrical spark travelling the neural motorway, so it can be dulled by a repetitive approach. So vary your starting procedure and explore new ways. Move up slowly from his ankles while keeping eye contact. You teasingly strip the clothes off looking at him as though you can hardly contain yourself, while touching him everywhere. You slide your body against his, then downward now so your genitals are positioned over his knee while you toy with his inner thigh and pubic area. You run your fingers through his pubic hair and over his balls slowly and you lick the tip of his penis softly while gazing into his eyes showing your desire. Touch his balls and under the balls and in between bum. Run your tongue around them. Move up to lick his shaft. The lower side of a man's shaft has many nerves running making it the more sensitive side. Take the whole shaft in your mouth (or as much as you can). Do not worry about how deep you can go. It will improve with practice. The most important idea is how you manipulate your tongue. Begin with the sides of the shaft and zigzag through. With your tongue, press the dimple where the shaft meets the balls. Try to twirl your tongue around the shaft switching between clockwise and anti clockwise. Once you reach the ring beneath the tip swirl your tongue around it and press the tip. Go up and down like this a few times. Switch between fast and slow motions. He will be at loss of words!

Secret 14: Sexual Positions

Different sexual positions trigger different kind of sensation as the penetration from each angle touch unique pleasure spot inside a woman. So do not wait for a man to suggest, be enthusiastic to try different positions for your own benefit. It is like going to an ice-cream shop, you will not know your favourite till you try them all. Do not restrict sex in the bedroom only. Pull your man to make passionate love on sofa, kitchen counter top, bath tub or any other place that is stable enough to take the load. Sex is not only for a man to initiate and woman to put up with.

Secret 15: Dealing With the Morning After

As an escort I often had overnight bookings. On my first overnight booking with 'Mike', the main thought that ran through my mind is that he will turn around and see me without makeup...yikes!! However it was not a problem that morning or any morning thereafter.

Actually a lot of men prefer women with natural look. My head was on Mike's shoulder, long brown hair fell loosely on his chest. I touched Mike gently and sensually to which he woke up and said, "Gosh you look lovely and fresh". Then we made love. There is no better way to start a day than making love first thing in the morning, especially after you have cuddled and spooned all night. Needless to say that I was smiling all day long despite the London weather in October.

Secret 16: Velvet Glove

Contrary to popular belief, modern men like intelligent, strong and independent woman who is not afraid to speak her mind and explore her sexuality. However make sure that you do not come across as harsh or accusatory. Try to put a positive spin on your thoughts. Such as, instead of telling him "Oh you never look into my eyes when we make love" put it across like "I love it when you look into my eyes when we make love". You will notice that he is much more willing to comply and make you happy. One reason men like escorts is that there is no complication or accusation in the experience. Pointing finger will only make a man defensive. Besides it is love that you are looking for in bed, not war, so, keep the iron fist at bay and bring on the velvet glove. In fact buy some lovely silk/satin long gloves from lingerie shop today and wear them (only them) in bed.

Secret 17: Know When to Give Space

It is common for a woman to think that if she keeps an eye on her man then she can have the object of desire all to herself. However, the more you ask questions the more evasive a man is likely to become. Going through his blackberry while he is in the shower might give you insight, but do you really want to him to return the favour?? Besides interrogating will not make him give up his flirting, it will only make him better at hiding things from you. Lots of men even go to the extent of keeping a separate mobile number just for the purpose of contacting ladies.

I know, it is easier said than done, and we all have made this mistake some point in our lives, but know that you cannot lock a human being in cage if he does not want to stay. Sooner or later he will go on in the direction he originally planned and you would be left with an empty cage. In fact the more freedom you give him the more he would offer to spend time with you… and that is true quality time.

Besides you do not want to go through the everyday stress and pain of holding on to an unavailable, slippery man in the first place.

Secret 18: Be Greedy

Sex can be addictive. The more you have it, the more you would want it. The longer a woman abstains from sex, the lower libido is likely to be, resulting in dryness, discomfort in sex etc. The longer a man abstains from sex the worse his performance becomes. Research shows sex is also one of the major factors of happiness in life.

So have a vivid imagination and keep up the practice. Besides sex burns up calories, for the days you want to skip gym. It is common misconception that ageing brings end to sex life. I know couples who are well into their 80s but still eager to enjoy sex. My oldest client was 87 years old! Main point is not to stop the habit. On days you are not having sex, fantasize about sex… unashamedly. Make 'rolling in bed with a little bit of honey' your favourite daily breakfast!

Secret 19: Learn to Let Go

Men can separate sex from emotion far easily than women can. Therefore being upset and worried about a disagreement you had ten days back is of no use. You cannot take back the argument you had, but clinging on to it and dragging it to bed, will only make things worse. Most possibly your partner has already forgotten about it and moved on, so the next best step would be to not pout in bed about it. In fact bed is the perfect place to kiss and make up! It is commonly miscalculated that emotional blackmails through sexual withdrawals can bring a person where you want him to be. But eventually the only person missing out on sex would be the individual pouting in bed. The other half has probably slipped out…

Secret 20: Fantasize

Perhaps the most stimulating and powerful element of sex is to FANTASIZE! All sexual thoughts originate in brain. Fantasies are wishful thinking, which you imagine just as you like it, with no one else to put up with. Fantasizing is the best way to get in the mood of sex, which you can do anytime and anywhere. Do not feel guilty about having wild fantasies. No matter how wild it is, it can always be played out with the right person. Your partner would be eager to play them out with you more often than you think. If you feel some fantasy is absolutely no-no with your partner, then do not share. Just play them in your mind while you are having sex. That itself will be the source of astonishing orgasms.

In the following chapter, I talk about thirty of the fantasies my clients have disclosed to me or I have shared with them. These might give you insight on male fantasies and some ideas for raunchy evenings without TV. In fact if you like all these fantasies then you will have one for each day of the month.

FANTASIES:

Fantasy 1: Facials

Lots of men like to see their semen on the face of the woman they are with. One of the common request I get as an escort is to cum on my face, lips even hair. My client 'Adam' is particularly fond of facial cum. He stops the intercourse when he just about reaching the climax and climbs up on me. I grab his balls and let him shoot all over my face and hair (make sure to close the eyes as semen causes burning in the eyes). Then you lick it off your lips if you want to taste the semen as the sight of a woman licking his cum off her face gives a man unreserved satisfaction.

Fantasy 2: Nude Body to Body Massage

As a qualified masseur, I often got requests from my clients to massage them. 'Martin', who has a stressful job in the city, comes to see me once a week for stress relief. We take our clothes off and I sit on his bum. I massage aromatic lavender oil all over his back alternating between firm pressure and sensuous touch. Lavender has natural relaxant properties. I begin in circular motion with his tense muscles around the shoulder bones and neck. Then I move my thumbs down the sides of the backbone and massage the lower back and sides. Once the stress relief part is over and the muscles are relaxed, I begin to do 'body-to-body massage'. From firm pressure I switch to gentle touching with my fingertips. Starting at the back I keep moving my fingers down around his highly sensitive bum, legs and feet. Then I softly kiss his whole back of the body while breathing heavily on him. The breathing enhances the sensual feeling. Afterwards, I lick and rub my body, especially breasts, up and down Martin's back and bum. Eventually after gentle torture, I turn him over and kiss his neck, flick his nipples with my tongue and bite them ever so gently. I put my breasts right on Martin's mouth for him to suck on. Then I slide down to rub my boobs all over his torso. I take his penis in between my breasts while kissing around nipples, bellybutton, maintaining seductive eye contact with him. I touch his feet, massaging the sole and the toes. Feet control the reflexology of the entire body, including sex organs. Hence massaging feet can be astonishingly relaxing and sensual experience. Areas around the ankle and around the wrist control the groin. Needless to say that massaging and kissing these zones can be erotic. These areas of body are often ignored but if you can wake up these secret areas, you will get a surprise reaction in your partner's eyes. Back of the knees and inside the elbows are two other hidden gems. Moving away from Martin's feet, I lie flat on my front, him on top of me and take him in from behind, a position perfect to touch my G-spot.

Fantasy 3: Bondage/ Domination

Most men enjoy being dominated in bed time to time. There is no absolute need to go all out hard core for this purpose. Just be armed with a cane or whip, handcuffs, blindfold, ankle ties and high heels. Make him kneel and beg in front of you. Then cuff his arms and ankles and slap him. Tell him how bad he has been and how much he deserves punishment then give him a kick and whip/ cane him. Sit on his face and make him taste you. Then put you feet on his face and make him lick your feet. Woman on top is the position to go with domination. The more adventurous can even buy furniture that is specially made for bondage and domination or you can even have a full-fledged dungeon if you find it satisfactory.

For the brave hearts out there, there is more extreme form of bondage. 'Peter', one of my clients loves to be submissive. I get dressed in a policewoman's uniform and black high heel boots. I handcuff Peter and tie his ankles so he is completely in my hands. I put clamps on his nipples and apply pressure. I then tie his balls and penis with a harness and make him kneel before me to kick his balls. He moans in pain but pleasure is written all over him at the same time. The harness prolongs a man's erection by keeping blood inside the penis. Some men wears the harness because they have erectile difficulties, but Peter likes it because of the particular sensation of tightness and engorgement that the ring provides. I then make him lie on my wooden floor face down and walk on him with my high heeled boots. I grab Peter by his hair, whip him on his butt and tell him to lick my boots, which he obliges.

He then begs me to put him out of his misery and promises to obey my every wish. I get on top of him and take him inside me till he finishes. In orgasm, the testicles usually retract toward the body before ejaculation. A ring around the balls intensifies the sensation of orgasm by forcing the testicles to stay away from the body. Peter screams as he reaches intense orgasm.

Fantasy 4: Sex in Shower/Bath

I prepare a hot bubble bath with aromatic candles lit up all around the bathroom (switching off all other light) to create a magically romantic atmosphere to enjoy sex to the fullest when 'Sean' comes over. Sometimes we are adventurous enough to make love in the bath tub, however, if you find having sex in bath tub too complicated then move on to more comfortable bed after the sexy bath, using the bath tub as just a foreplay ground. A steamy session of foreplay or full fledged lovemaking under running shower with invigorating shower gel foaming on your bodies is equally stimulating and a popular foreplay. The sight of water streaming down your face, breasts and back will drive men crazier than lions on heat!!

Fantasy 5: Role Playing: Secretary/ Colleague

Men often fantasize about making love in the office, purely because it is risky and prohibited. I visit ‘Stephan’ in his penthouse, one of my clients who flies into London from Belgium almost every week for work. I was wearing a white shirt with few top buttons undone, tight black skirt, sexy hold ups/ stockings and high heels, I walk into his study room where he waits for me and sit on the desk with my legs crossed and titillate him. I run my legs against his, unzip his trousers and tickle him with my feet. He lifts my skirt up, moves my sexy butterfly knickers to a side and goes down on me. I get on my knees and take him in my mouth. Finally we make love with me sitting on him on the chair. Bending over the desk and having sex from behind is also a position that goes with this role playing

Fantasy 6: Uniforms and Stockings

Uniforms of all sorts are high on men's fantasy list. Nurse, masseur, air hostess, maid, playboy bunny are the easiest to tickle men's sexual instinct. Two of the highest requests I got for dressing up were, nurse's uniform and corset, thong, suspenders and stockings with high heels. Upon 'Jonathon's' request on the phone to wear a nurse's uniform for him, I put on my tight little white nurse's uniform with very high ankle tie heels. My nails were painted deep red and hair under the nurse headpiece was tied loosely. Jonathon likes me to unzip my uniform halfway to expose my bare breasts partially and take my white lacy thongs off. I then sit on top of him on my sofa and kiss him while he touches me. Then we have sex doggy-style keeping my uniform on while having sex. Uniforms are quite reasonably priced to buy and, most uniforms do not take much effort to put on, yet, they will allow you to rank very high on your man's fantasy meter.

Stockings, suspenders and corset similarly are considered exceptionally erotic by men. This was one of my favourite outfits for incall (when gentlemen visited me). It always served the purpose right on spot. If you find suspenders and stockings too much a hassle then you can try Basque, thong and hold-ups, which are easier and faster options but equally high on hot-o-meter. Corset or Basque hides physical imperfections by slimming the waistline and enhancing cleavage. It is the secret of forming an hour glass figure instantly. Stockings make legs look toned. Some men find it erotic to even rip off hold-ups/ stockings.

Fantasy 7: Taking Nude/ Semi Nude Pictures

Arrange a photo shoot with a professional photographer or have your partner take sexy nude and semi nude photos. Watching you undress fully or put on sexy lingerie and high heels only to pose for photography will put both of you in mood. Men love to look at sexy photos and fantasize, so why not make them your own photos? Some of the professional escort photographers take and airbrush photos for a reasonable price. Put them in a private album and use it with your partner anytime you want reference. He will even admit looking at them and fantasizing about you when you are not around. My client ‘Tom’ always looks at my album as a part of his foreplay even though I am with him in person.

Fantasy 8: Going On a Date without Underwear

Once ‘David’ invited me to go to a dinner date with him. I got ready wearing a fitted black dress, stilettos, choker necklace, perfume and no underwear. David picks me up in his Porsche. Halfway on our way, I softly whisper into his ear about what I was ‘not wearing’. Needless to say that he had only one thought all through the date. I ran my heels up his calves under the table middle of our dinner. David told me how naughty I was, I could tell that his mind was running wild. We could not wait to come home and make love.

Fantasy 9: Touching Each Other in Car

On our way to one night out to a black tie event, I run my hands on and in between David's legs. I let him feel my smooth legs and slip his hand in my black sparkly evening gown to feel my incredibly sexy pearl thong. He ran his fingers through the pearls, the sensation so intense I had to bite my lips. There was a sense of intense anticipation yet both of us had to wait for the moment. At the party we found a quite place away for some discreet foreplay once again. David grabbed me, kissed my lips and neck while running his fingers through my hair, there was no better aphrodisiac than touch. I dug my fingers in his hair and back, he looked so incredible sexy in his black tuxedo. We returned to the party but we had only one thing in our minds. By the time we returned home, we were too desperate to stop the 'torture' and rip each other clothes off. David moved the pearls of my thong with his teeth to taste me and so, on we went in our own world, to make love.

Fantasy 10: Fireplace

'Desmond' whisked me away to a Spa Boutique Resort on Scottish highlands for a Valentine's weekend. Our room smelled of the fresh pink lilies that were placed in the vase and we had the view of distant mountains. The wooden four poster king sized bed with plush pillows faced a roaring fireplace. A regal painting hung above it and soft rug were laid in front of the fireplace. We switched off all the lights and the fire of the fireplace lit the room up. The curtains were left open and twinkling stars were visible in the distant. We opened a bottle of champagne and sat down on the rug close to the fireplace. I wore ivory silk long low cut lingerie with thigh high slit and lace trimming. Desmond kissed me ever so softly on my lips and neck. He ran his hands through my hair and whispered how beautiful I looked. I pulled him close to me and kissed him deeply. Then I pushed him down on the rug opened his robe and sat on him. I leaned down to kiss Desmond on the lips and he pulled me close to him. I laid on him while he softly touched my bum and back over my silk lingerie. 'Oh Desmond, you smell so nice', I moaned in utter pleasure. He lifted my lingerie and his hand touched my bare thighs. 'You are so smooth' he said. I spread my thighs a little for him to feel my moist inside. He knew how much I was eager for him to penetrate me. I slowly got up, sat on top on Desmond and leaned forward. My hair flipped on his face, he grabbed it pushed it back and we made love looking in to each others eyes.

Fantasy 11: Masturbation

'Connor' likes to watch me touch my body and pleasure myself. I touch myself over my mesh short dress. The see through dress clings to my body and shows off my assets. I tease my nipples with my fingers then I slip my hands under my dress, visible from outside. I touch myself till I cum while maintaining eye contact with Connor. Masturbation is not a mean to please yourself but also an effective foreplay. Watching a woman undress and touching her own body and making herself reach orgasm through masturbation is tremendously motivating for a man. Most women find it difficult to relax and let her man watch pleasuring herself in an ultimate way. But remember there is nothing to feel shy about, as men would purely focus on the sexual act and not on minute faults on your body. By the time you satisfy yourself on round one, be ready for next round as your man would be rock hard.

Fantasy 12: Sex Toys

Use of sex toys are safe yet fun way to spice up your sex life. Vibrators, dildos, clit stimulators, cock rings, genital harnesses, flavoured condoms, and play-lubricants can all be part of your sex life to enhance and stimulate your pleasure zones. Watching sex toys being used can also boost the sexual desire. As an escort I always stocked up on flavoured condom because they made giving blowjob tastier on occasions I did not to taste the man directly. It also overrides physical odour lots of men naturally have around their genitals. If you, like me, do not fancy the 'man-odour-hood', you would find flavoured condoms heaven sent. Lubricants have a nice warm feel to them and it is much easier to get a man hard with warming lubricant than without. 'Paul' and I always used sex toys to enhance our exclusive time together. I put on warming lubricant on his penis and balls with both hands immediately he became hard. Then I slid my fingers in me instantly I felt a warm, tingling sensation inside my vagina. I picked up the vibrator lying next to the bed and pushed it inside me as Paul watched in ecstasy. As I lost myself enjoying the throbbing motions of the vibrator, Paul kept on kissing my body to add on to the pleasure for both us.

Fantasy 13: Mothering

As prohibited as it might sound to some people, lots of men have fantasy to dress up as babies and go through nappy changing, breast feeding, i.e., all the mother and baby role playing acts while you baby talk him. It is surely not everyone's cup of tea, but give it a try in case it remotely interests you.

Fantasy 14: Cross Dressing

Lots of heterosexual men like to dress up as women in private. Lots of escorts specialize in clients coming to see them with special request to be dressed up as a woman. They are a heterosexual professional man with no unusual past yet dressing themselves as women is an act of sexual indulgence. If this fantasy excites you and your partner then sit him down by the dressing table and apply basic foundation, lipstick and mascara on him. Put a Marilyn Monroe style blonde bob wig on him. Then make him slide on silk corset with padding and matching knickers. Finally, let the man slip on a pair of red high heel shoes. Some days when both of you have time, you can even paint his nails and toes as special treat. Call him by a woman's name. When the makeover session finishes, allow your man to walk around in the flat and admire his 'other-self' in the full mirror.

Fantasy 15: Anal

Anal sex is increasingly becoming popular with both men and women. One reason is that the anus is considered to yield more tactile pleasure for the penis, being tighter than the vagina.

A lot of women think that only gay men want be penetrated anally but the truth is lots of heterosexual men are anally aroused and like the use of strap-on by their women. In fact, it is a man's way of being subservient to the woman. Moreover, due to the proximity of the prostate gland to the rectum, it has been suggested that males may achieve greater satisfaction in this manner than females. The prostate gland, also known as a "male G-spot" can be stimulated during anal intercourse. Stimulation of the prostate gland can result in pleasurable sensations and can lead to a distinct type of orgasm in some cases. The prostate is located next to the rectum and is the larger, more developed.

Anal sex need not involve penile insertion. The active partner (man or woman) may use fingers rather than a penis/dildo. The use of the mouth and tongue on the anus is called rimming or analingus which can also be highly erotic and sensuous to some.

Fantasy 16: First Love

Some men, especially from oriental cultures, like the idea of being with a virgin or talk about losing virginity. Wearing schoolgirl uniform and hair in a ponytail compliments this fantasy. Talking about how excited you are and how tight your pussy is turns on men.

Fantasy 17: Sex in the Open/ Balcony/ Tent

Sex driven by exhibitionism is a turn on for people for its risky nature. Stripping and acts of lovemaking in the balcony, garden or anywhere in the open can be a turn on. 'Robert' my adventurous male amour once invited me to a music festival, where we spent the night in a tent. After the hustle and bustle settled down, we crawled in our tent. Robert was keen on taking my turquoise strapless top off (I was wearing nothing underneath) and kissing my entire upper body. He then slid my cropped tight jeans off and nibbled on my ankles and calves. I forgot all about the surroundings and gave in to his temptations. I took Robert's clothes off and we started our journey to risky sex. I bit my lips realizing that I moaned in pleasure just a little too loud. Robert throbbed away whispering naughty comments in to my ears. I put my both arms around him as we both reached for orgasm. It was the first time I ever had sex in such risky condition, with people just outside, which made it all the more exciting.

Fantasy 18: Watersports

Watersports is sexual fantasy regarding urination. Men often request escorts to urinate all over on their body. Having tea or ice tea usually is a quick and easy way to fulfil this fantasy. The man usually reaches orgasm by giving himself a hand-job at the same time of receiving watersports. I once had a man whose fantasy was to feel a woman while she pees in her knickers.

Fantasy 19: Threesome/Group

We all know that most men like to watch two women touch each other. However in modern days, lots of heterosexual couples are inviting a third person in their sex life for stimulation and more often it is the woman's idea. I have lots of couples as clients who see me for special occasions such as birthdays and anniversaries.

The first couple I ever did was 'Katie and Steve'. They drove to London to celebrate their wedding anniversary. On the phone Katie mentioned that she enjoys women just as much as her husband does. I joined them for a drink in their hotel bar wearing a black fitted dress, pearls, stilettos and sexy lingerie underneath. Katie was wearing a white fitted shirt and tight jeans, she had her blonde hair up in a French knot showing off the diamonds earrings she just got as anniversary gift from Steve. Steve was dressed smart casual and together they made a very attractive couple. After the drinks we all went up to the room.

Katie and I kissed passionately with deep tongue while Steve watched. A woman's lips are far more tender and soft to kiss and we immediately felt the chemistry. I unbuttoned Katie's shirt revealing her white lace bra and smooth skin. We kissed again and touched each other all over. I turned around and asked Steve to unzip my dress exposing my black bra and thong. I returned Steve the favour by kissing him on the mouth and neck and taking his shirt off … he smelled delicious. Katie got on her knees, took Steve's jeans off and started giving him blowjob while I put my arms around Katie and played with her nipples and kissed her soft back. Katie stood up, I took her jeans and kickers off and pulled both of them to bed. We ladies flicked and sucked on each others' breasts followed by Steve sucking and going down on both of us. I kissed Katie upwards from ankle to thighs and then finally licking her moist clit till she reached climax and moaned in ultimate bliss. I then turned to Steve and started sucking on his already hard cock and balls while Katie laid on the bed dazed. I was still horny and Steve entered me from behind and pleasured me. He then turned to Katie and made love to her till he ejaculated in her.

After a few moments of catching out breath, all three of us giggled and Katie said that she could not have asked for a better anniversary experience!

Fantasy 20: Bikini Wax Designs

If you like the look of delightful surprise when your partner takes your clothes off, try getting a super sexy bikini line wax. The latest trend in body art is decorating one's waxed private parts with crystals in various styles. After waxing off almost all of the hair in the bikini area, body gems or crystals are stuck on to the skin in various shapes. The most popular designs are hearts and the tiffany box which is to wax the pubic hair into a square design. The landing strip is also popular for decoration - a thin line of hair is left un-waxed and crystals placed on sides.

Many salons are now offering a choice of templates to create special bikini designs, such as the made-tomeasure heart-shaped bikini wax which is available at many salons across the world. Then to show off your sexy bikini line, slip on a pearl thong. My favourite thong is made of black lace panel around the waist with a single white pearl string running from the front to back, so the undercarriage is only covered by the pearl string.

Fantasy 21: Paid Sex

Paid sex or sex with escort itself is an extremely erotic thought for people due to the forbidden nature of the act. Thought of an unknown person getting ready for a discreet sex session arouses many men (and women). So have your man call you as a stranger, to make the 'deal' such as fixing a time, rate and place (you can also do the calling if the thought of call boys appeal to you). The place you decide to meet up can be your home but it is even more thrilling if it a discreet hotel room is booked for two anonymous people to meet up. Wear something sexy and greet him with a lusty look when he rings the doorbell. Open a bottle of wine at which point he would slip you the 'envelope'. Once the 'transaction' has been completed, feel free to rip each others clothes off and have sex anyway you prefer, but it might be good to experience as raw primal sex.

Fantasy 22: Cigar

Famously known for the event in 'The Oval Office', cigar fantasy is actually quiet common. Lot of men have admitted to me that a woman giving them a blowjob while he smokes a cigar is wonderfully erotic.

Fantasy 23: Leather / Spandex

The smell of the leather and the riplling noises it produces is often an erotic stimulus for lots of men. Leather uniforms are also fetishized. The combination of leather with the uniform's symbolism of authority and power. The feel of tight leather or spandex garments are also be viewed as a kind of sexual bondage. One reason why spandex and other tight fabrics may be fetishised is that the garment gives the illusion of second skin. 'John' always requests me to wear spandex almost see-through bodysuit for him. He likes to rub and lick the bodysuit as if it is my skin. The bodysuit hugs every part of my body making it as sexy as being naked. I keep the bodysuit on through out the foreplay…

Fantasy 24: Mirrors

Making love facing mirrors are tremendously erotic as you see both bodies and the act. It is like watching pornography where the actors are yourselves! Mirrors on the ceiling or on the walls would reflect your bodies pressed against each other in erotic positions and enhance the stimulation. Dim the lights if you feel you need a confidence boost as soft lighting gives body a flattering look. Try it, it is one of my favourites!

Fantasy 25: Food Fetish

Dripping honey or whipping cream all over your sensuous parts does not happen only in the movies. You can have it right in your bed too. You can pour chocolate sauce all over your breasts and have your man lick it off. Return the favour by pouring some on him and sensually swirl it all off. This way, even if you don't like his taste, the chocolate sauce would make things tastier! Men being visual, will love to watch you lick him like he saw in the porno movies and enjoy.

'Jack' and I once celebrated his promotion by opening a bottle of champagne and pouring it all over our bodies. The champagne rolled down my breast and nipples down my body all the way. Then Jack licked it all off of me while I returned the favour.

Fantasy 26: Phone Sex

Chatting with someone with a sexy voice describing how much you crave for each others touch, sharing vividly what you are wearing at the moment, how you are touching yourself is one of the top fantasies. Have sex over the phone when you are away from each other and hold on to that thought for the next time you can do it for real. Sometimes expressing your fantasies over the phone might be easier than in person.

Fantasy 27: Webcam

In modern technology days, sex over the webcam is one of the most popular businesses. If your partner is away on business trip, and you are missing each other, then webcam is the answer. Put on something sexy and tease your partners for first few minutes. Then slowly take one piece off at a time. Lick you fingers and touch your body very gently. Tell your partner what you would like to do to him and what you like him to do to you. Then start the masturbation. Use vibrators or other toys if you fancy.

Fantasy 28: Foot/ Shoe Fetish

One of the common fetishes I have come across while entertaining gentlemen, is foot and shoe fetish. I like to wear nice shoes, my feet are neatly pedicured and my toes always painted. 'Richard' was one of the callers who loved to worship feet. Licking boots, sucking the heels of stilettos, kissing toes everything suited him. He used to sit on the floor while I put my feet on his shoulders. He would kiss my heels, suck on my toes one by one. I touch myself while he sucks on the sides of my feet and he gives himself a hand-job. He then ejaculated on my feet and shoes.

Fantasy 29: Body Art

The ancient skill of painting the body permanently or temporarily is not only a form of art but also sexually provocative for some. At first painted body does not seem nude, but slowly it is realized that it is only paint that is covering the nude body. It moulds the entire body with a touch of mystery and imagination. Shape of every part is understood, every movement accentuated. You can paint a whole bodysuit on your body or paint something little like a tattoo.

Fantasy 30: Stranger at the Bar

My regular client 'Andrew' and I planned a mystery date with at a trendy bar. I was dressed in a backless black cocktail dress with diamante straps and diamante stilettos with matching clutch bag. Underneath I wore my favourite butterfly shaped thong with diamante strings (Andrew had no clue to what I was wearing). I arrived at the bar few minutes before Andrew, and sat on a high chair at the bar. I ordered a glass of champagne and avoided eye contact with all the other men in the bar. After few minutes Andrew entered and stood across the bar from me and ordered champagne for himself. We made sultry eye contact, shortly after he sent across a drink to me. I rose the glass and smiled at him. He came over to me and introduced himself and said how beautiful I looked. He lightly touched my bare back with his fingertips sending shivers down my spine. I could feel the chemistry instantly. To reciprocate the interest I gently touched his fingers with mine, complimenting his cufflinks. Our eyes locked, we flirted and kissed passionately at the bar, and decided to go to my place.

We could not keep our hands off of each other in the car. I put my arms around Andrew and he kissed me upon reaching my place. We started to undress there and then, raw passion driving us both into a state of bliss…

ADVICE FOR MEN:

Almost every man I have ever been to bed with asked me about his performance quality. Knowing that as an escort I have extensive experience, lots of men seem to reason that if they get my seal of approval then they are set for Lady Luck in this life. Thus I thought I would give some tips to men on how to get your women jump on you when you come home.

Advice 1: Art of Courtship

First impression is usually the decisive impression. Like in the world of business, make your first impression count in romance and courtship, because you may never get a second chance. It is a pity that old fashioned art of courtship seem like a forgotten art nowadays. Despite the modern lifestyle and equal rights, most women still inclined to the idea of old fashioned courtship of flower paved invitation. When you have a woman in mind you want to ask out, spend some time being an absolute gentleman to her before you make your move as a warm up. Women put high importance on making the first date (or any date) special. Taking the lady of choice around the corner without making specific plans or reservation is not likely to leave a lasting impression on her mind. Whether you decide to make a reservation to take your date to a posh restaurant for a candlelit dinner or make a lovely home cooked meal, make sure it expresses that you have planned and made an effort to please her. A woman will appreciate and remember the gesture. Feel free to ask her about her preferences, if you are unsure.

How you behave on your first date gives women preview of what kind of man you would be for her. So make her first date with you the best first date she would ever have, or better yet, the last first date she would ever have. Showing interest in her hobbies, opening the door for her, assisting her putting her coat on are few of the small details that will get you high on her book.

Another excellent idea would be refraining from looking around or flirting with other women while you are on a date with someone as it is highly disrespectful, and women neither forgive nor forget such actions. Women have sharp eyes hence, what men consider one discreet 'innocent' glance, can be detected by women.

Drink only in moderation. Your date will not feel safe with a man who cannot handle his drinks. Excessive drinking will only make you make a fool of yourself. Taking chemical substance to enhance 'performance' is another no-no. It will make your mind focus on sex so much that you will not concentrate on the woman. Would it not be a pity if at the end, despite the chemically boosted hours long marvellous hard-on, you do not get 'any' anyway.

Keep your place tidy at all times. It would be ironic if you manage to get your hot date in your place only to discover that she is put off by the mess. So do not be caught unprepared. A clean home is a sign of a well organized, stable, mature man who can take care of himself.

Advice 2: Do Not Be Desperate

When you meet a woman for the first time, no matter how long you have not had sex, do not prowl over her like dog on heat to show your desperation when you first meet a woman. Desperation indicates that you have been repeatedly unsuccessful in your ventures and automatically works as a turn-off. Be a charming gentleman and show interest in her. Compliment her on her looks without staring down at her cleavage, groping her bum or tugging on her dress straps. After the date, drop her at her place and let the woman decide if she wants to invite you in or not for tea (we all know that tea is not the only thing on offer). If you corner a woman and say ‘my place or yours’, she is likely to say ‘neither’ and even worse, not go out with you the second time around. Banish the thought “what is the point of paying her food bill if I cannot get lucky in the first go”. It is always better to let a woman make the first sexual move, since you have no chance of rejection then.

Besides, a man's performance is usually unsatisfactory when he is desperate. Surely, you do not want your hot date to remember you as "the guy who finished in two minutes"…

Advice 3: Attention to Detail

Women pay far more attention to detail than men think. So please do not put on socks with holes or show up with nails that look like cat's claws with dirt under them. Your date would probably get a mysterious 'emergency' phone call that there has been a leak in her flat or her best friend is in hospital and she has to go, immediately. Even if you are with a woman for a long time, do not let your dressing style slide when you are with her. Do not abstain from shaving on weekends, remember that's the time your partner gets to notice you the most. We all like to wake up to morning lovemaking on weekends and role around the bed in laze but scruffy cheeks are not pleasant to feel against face let alone the more sensuous parts.

When you take a lady out for a date, make sure you keep the audience in mind when dress. It is the small things in dressing that make the difference. Cufflinks, wrist watch, shoes, socks and above all nice cologne make the biggest impression.

Advice 4: Always Ask

If you are with a woman for the first time, please ask before you try something adventurous. Do not push your fingers up in her genitals without asking. You will get a very angry slap on the wrist, literally. Instead do the things she enjoys the most, be sensuous and play around with her. You will notice that after a while your woman would be suggesting far more adventurous things than you ever imagined! The best sex I have ever had were with men who were not in a hurry first time around.

Advice 5: Be Gentle

I know that the idea to bed-breaking sex appeals to many men, but believe me you should always start gently and slowly. Take time to get her to warm up to you. Give her a little massage, kiss her neck all the down her back. Common misperception is that the nipples are the only sensuous zone of the breasts, but do not forget that the side and just under the breasts are also highly sensuous hidden gems. You can discover them by stretching her arms up and kissing the sides of her breasts and under the nipples, then flicking the nipples with your tongue. Biting on her neck and nipples will make her scream but not in a favourable way. If she wanted bite marks she would be going out with Dracula or mad dogs.

When you go down on a woman, do not dive in straight away. Instead move further down where she least expects it and kiss her ankles, then move up to kiss the inner thighs and back of the knees to get her craving for more. Make her wait and build up the momentum, hear her say that she cannot wait anymore. Then slowly taste her, by now she would be dripping moist, moaning with pleasure and ready for bed breaking sex more than you wanted it in the first place.

Advice 6: Smell Good (Specially the Private Parts)

Sometimes smell can be a more important factor in attraction than the look itself. Do not forget the smell in your private parts. If you expect a woman to perform the most amazing blowjob, then make sure that she does not run to the bathroom after you take your pants off. Please wash yourself after you cum, every time. Good blowjobs just do not happen if a woman is holding her breath! Next night when she goes to bed, if pleasant, your smell would still be lingering and she would be fantasizing about you. But if unpleasant, you would be in her washing machine. Which way do you want her to remember you?

Advice 7: Be Sensuous

Touch a woman very gently just with the fingertip. Kiss her softly, shoving your tongue down her throat will not do the trick. Focus on shoulder and neck, back, nipple, sides of the breasts, inner thighs, feet, and bum. While using tongue, gently flick or run through. There is no need to press her ribcages together or treating her breasts like potatoes under masher. If she wants it stronger, she would tell you. Grabbing her head and shoving your 'best' part in her mouth is also a no-no. You will not get quality blowjob out of brute force. Instead let her take the lead, you might enjoy letting go and relaxing more than you think.

Advice 8: Start with an Easy Position

Begin with a position that is easy for the woman. Leave the woman to choose a position of her liking. Do not bend her down and feel free to take her any way you like it. Once she is enjoying herself, she will be more open to adventurous ideas. Once you are inside her, stroke gently at first, and then build up the speed and force. In fact chances are that the lady would ask you to do it harder.

But if you start out in a very rough manner, she will have thrush the next day to remember you by.

Advice 9: Be Genuine

Sometimes the most romantic things are not dozen roses or expensive candlelit dinners. Instead it can be simple gestures like feeding her pet, giving her a quick phone call in between your meetings, ironing her shirt when she is in a hurry, giving her a back massage when she is tired (without expecting sex in return) or shoving snow off her car one cold morning. Trust me you would be collecting much higher reward points from afterwards from her than your Harrods Reward Card. Romantic gestures do not have to be make-believe or high maintenance all the time. Just make sure it comes from the heart as women are very intuitive and they can always tell.

One afternoon, while having lunch, a friend said that he had rearranged his entire day's schedule and drove for an hour just to have this little bit of precious time with me before he was going away for a business trip. Among all the pretentious attention I receive, that sincere comment stood out. After lunch I gave him a kiss on his lips and he went off to catch his flight…

Advice 10: Be Tidy

Please do NOT expect women to feel sexy towards you if she has been picking up your dirty socks and de-cluttering for you everyday. Any sexual thought she might have for you would be gone by the time she has cleaned shaving leftover of off the sink and smelled your dirty laundry all day. If you try to be tidy and share the household chores, you will gain affection and appreciation from your woman. The more you make an effort to please your woman, the more she would enjoy her time with you. Besides, we all know that a tired woman in bed is no fun at all. You want her to have some energy left for you, don't you? A minute spent in organizing your surroundings is an hour earned for yourself.

Common misconception is that relationships break up because of entrance of a third person. However the truth is most relationships are already in near break up stage due to problem between the partners, while the third person is only a coincidence to enter the picture. In my escorting career, I have listened to many peoples' wide ranging problems. Men and women spend way too much time thinking that they are from different planets. Whereas the truth is men and women are actually diving towards the same ambition. Both men and women think that the opposite sex is a mystery, only because we do not take the time to listen and understand how similar the opposite sex is to us. Members of the two sexes are perhaps no more different than each person is different in own unique way. As the society no longer divides boys and girls, women do just as well as men in math and workplace while most of the top chefs, creative artists and designers are heterosexual men. In fact, participation of both genders has only made the workplace more productive.

We can try the same method of success in our sex life. If we only agree to let our guards down and accept that life should be left simple. Spending time analyzing every comment, silence and laughter will drive you both apart. The faster you let go of a disagreement the faster things will move on and less complication it would cause. People accept criticism from their friends positively as good advice. However same criticism coming from a partner can become offensive. Take things as they are, and do not try to unearth hidden agenda that does not exist. Men complain of womens' shopping habits and women complain of mens' love for sports, leading to disagreement. However each complaining of habits that they do not find interesting in their own terms. So are we really different, or are we just very similar? If you begin to believe that your partner fails to understand you because of gender gap, then eventually you will focus on differences and ignore the similarities. Stop and accept the fact that two people are bound to have dissimilarities because we are all unique. Before you hold the gender issue responsible for all your intimate life problems, think of all the homosexual couples who are having just as much complications in their love life despite belonging to the same sex.

Assuming you understand the root of every problem is often the problem itself. Ask and discuss what your partner's needs and desires are. Give your partner a feeling that you are behind him or her on their decision. This does not necessarily mean agreeing with one another all the time. Realistically, no two people will agree on all occasions. What it does mean is treating your partner in a way that shows that you trust and respect your partner. Emotional support involves accepting your partner's differences and not insisting that they meet your needs only in the precise way you want them met. Find out how your partner chooses to show his or her love for you and do not impose criteria. Whenever you are willing to spend time with anybody, make the effort to turn it into quality time, it is the only type of time that counts.

Insisting that your partner spend all of his or her time with you, forcing that they give up their friends and drop hobbies for you, ask for your approval on the clothes they wear, power struggle to make all the decisions on how you spend your vacation together, making them feel guilty when they spend time alone or with their families, making sure you win all the arguments are all signs of emotional demands leading to people growing apart. If you are miserable in your own life, and looking for a partner to soak up the misery for you to make you happy, the minute they leave your life you will return to the melancholy self again. Partners can only share your joy and sorrow but they should never be the sole creator of it. Partnership is an external element in life that can enhance the lifestyle, but life should neither depend upon it nor confine to it.

So let us strive to make all our relationships in life assets, not liabilities.

www.ingramcontent.com/pod-product-compliance
Lightning Source LLC
Chambersburg PA
CBHW031002090426
42737CB00008B/650

* 9 7 8 1 8 4 7 4 7 3 9 7 4 *